Bb TRUMPET

CONCERT FAVORITES

Volume 2

Band Arrangements Correlated with
Essential Elements Band Method Book 1

ISBN 978-1-4234-0082-0

HAL•LEONARD®

7777 W. BLUEMOUND RD. P.O. BOX 13819 MILWAUKEE, WI 53213

00860170

BANDROOM BOOGIE

Bb TRUMPET

MICHAEL SWEENEY

BEETHOVEN'S NINTH

Bb TRUMPET

LUDWIG VAN BEETHOVEN
Arranged by PAUL LAVENDER

Lightly, with spirit

00860170

GALLANT MARCH

B♭ TRUMPET

MICHAEL SWEENEY

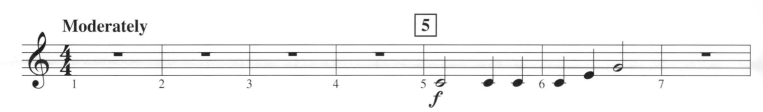

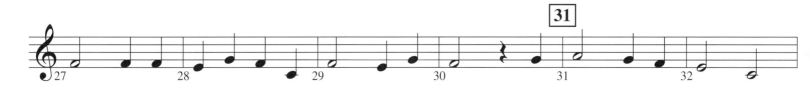

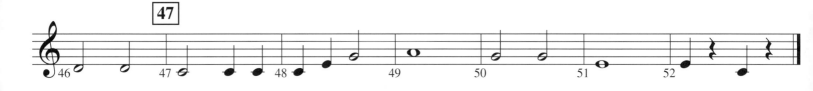

00860170

HIGH ADVENTURE

B♭ TRUMPET

PAUL LAVENDER

ROCK & ROLL – PART II
(The Hey Song)

Bb TRUMPET

Words and Music by
MIKE LEANDER and GARY GLITTER
Arranged by PAUL LAVENDER

00860170

AMAZING GRACE

Bb TRUMPET

Traditional American Melody
Arranged by PAUL LAVENDER

00860170

INFINITY
(Concert March)

Bb TRUMPET

JAMES CURNOW (ASCAP)

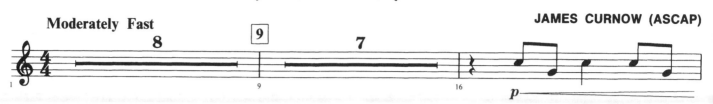

00860170

LATIN FIRE

B♭ TRUMPET

JOHN HIGGINS

LINUS AND LUCY

B♭ TRUMPET

By VINCE GUARALDI
Arranged by MICHAEL SWEENEY

00860170

(From The Paramount Motion Picture STAR TREK GENERATIONS)
THEME FROM "STAR TREK® GENERATIONS"

Bb TRUMPET

Music by DENNIS McCARTHY
Arranged by MICHAEL SWEENEY

AMERICAN SPIRIT MARCH

Bb TRUMPET

JOHN HIGGINS

GATHERING IN THE GLEN

B♭ TRUMPET

MICHAEL SWEENEY

00860170

THE LOCO-MOTION

Bb TRUMPET

Words and Music by
GERRY GOFFIN and CAROLE KING
Arranged by JOHN HIGGINS

Rock Style

00860170

ROYAL FIREWORKS MUSIC

B♭ TRUMPET

GEORGE FREDERIC HANDEL
Arranged by MICHAEL SWEENEY

(lower note opt.)

slowing

Moderately

(lower notes optional)

(lower notes optional)

slowing

00860170

SCARBOROUGH FAIR

Bb TRUMPET

Traditional English
Arranged by JOHN MOSS